MW01534913

Just Thinking

Just Thinking

By
Dr. Paula Sekeras

authorHOUSE®

AuthorHouse™
1663 Liberty Drive
Bloomington, IN 47403
www.authorhouse.com
Phone: 1-800-839-8640

© 2011 by Dr. Paula Sekeras. All rights reserved.

No part of this book may be reproduced, stored in a retrieval system, or transmitted by any means without the written permission of the author.

First published by AuthorHouse   10/14/2011

ISBN: 978-1-4634-3312-3 (sc)
ISBN: 978-1-4634-3311-6 (hc)
ISBN: 978-1-4634-3310-9 (ebk)

Library of Congress Control Number: 2011912148

Printed in the United States of America

Any people depicted in stock imagery provided by Thinkstock are models, and such images are being used for illustrative purposes only.
Certain stock imagery © Thinkstock.

Because of the dynamic nature of the Internet, any web addresses or links contained in this book may have changed since publication and may no longer be valid. The views expressed in this work are solely those of the author and do not necessarily reflect the views of the publisher, and the publisher hereby disclaims any responsibility for them.

Table of Contents

INTRODUCTION

Just Thinking About... originally began as my book of thoughts, an inspirational journal so to speak. Upon sharing what I had written with a few close friends, they encouraged me to have it published. Though it started as a modest book of verse, I decided to apply my knowledge of animal wisdom and incorporate some of my personal totems. I have included a few illustrations depicting natural settings to discern their meaning. For example the symbolism of the feathers on the front cover, remind me to be in the moment. The butterflies on the last page represent transformation. They represent a much deeper meaning to those who are partners with nature. I am a firm believer that a strong relationship with nature creates a good balance between one's body, mind, and spirit.

Within this book may *you* find your own reflections and inspiration.

Sending Light,
Love, and
Laughter,
Dr. Paula
Sekeras

CHAPTER ONE

Letting
In
Fulfilling
Experiences

If we become content with small portions of
joy in our life, then we have conditioned ourselves
to believe those obstacles and the mundane are
natural when, the opposite is true.
Joy must be a major priority to bring into our
life. When we can successfully master joyful
living, the mundane will appear in small portions
and obstacles won't seem so devastating.

6-98

Everything is made up of energy with a vibrational

force, plants, animals, rocks, trees, human beings, desires

and emotions, happy, sad, good and bad.

In order to achieve our desires we must match their

vibrational frequency.

When one can accomplish this, our desires will be met

because then we correspond to their vibration.

So keep your expectations high and experience

abundance and joy.

7-10

Challenges, tests, and obstacles that come in life are all

learning experiences that show us our strength, courage

and determination.

As long as we stay connected to our higher self through

these trials anything can be accomplished.

The power is within.

7-99

At night when the evening shadow is present,

what usually comes to mind is all of the I should've,

I could've, I wished I would've, and then we

have a tendency of projecting this unconsciously

into our tomorrows.

At the end of our day what we really need to focus

on is our accomplishments no matter how big or

small; our kind thoughts, words and deeds exchanged

with another, what made us feel good about ourselves,

and what brought us knowledge, joy, or laughter.

Some if not all should be present in each day. It is our

choice what we choose to recapture.

6-99

Sometimes when our energy is up and

we are having a Great Day, someone

comes along unexpectedly and ambushes

our heightened being. What we need to do

with ALL our might is not to give the person

or situation our power or energy . . . don't escalate

the drama and realize the person is displacing

their unwanted feelings and emotions on you.

Remember to set your boundaries, stay in your space

and don't let anyone take your power or

happiness away from you.

12-99

Freedom of being is accomplished when one

establishes their own comfort zone and takes

the necessary actions to maintain it.

It is then that we can break free of the past

conditioning and control drama's that life

has put on us.

At this plateau is where you will find life

was meant to be lived.

In complete harmony.

9-98

Sometimes we need to turn our "inside out"

in order to become our authentic self.

5-11

If we are not corresponding with our desires

we are missing our mark.

5-11

Time is one of our greatest stress factors.

I don't have enough time,

I'm out of time,

I'm on time,

I need more time,

You are on my time,

You've had enough time,

It's time for work . . . bed . . . to get up . . .

There just isn't enough time.

Enough time.

Just think for a moment . . . without time,

days, years, or lifetimes could be savored.

Sunrises, sunsets and seasons would be

our only time factors. As they once were.

People would be looked upon for their life experiences.

Always take time-out to just BE.

What a wonderful thought.

7-99

What is living?

Living is being able to condition ourselves

to stay in the moment.

No futurizing,

No past dwelling.

Literally Staying in the Moment!

9-99

If we always keep our back to the wind

We won't have the strength to meet some of life's

challenges that we are faced with.

Rather than reaching out to do something we love

especially, if it takes hard work, or disciplining

oneself. Instead we will just choose to be content

with whatever comes along.

By fearing the storm we will shy away from taking

a chance that could possibly enhance our life.

We will just let our negative fears consume us,

Instead of being positive and confident in ourselves

to accomplish what we need to.

(Continued)

When we refuse to go out on a cold snowy day,

we could be denying ourselves an exhilarating life

experience. Not realizing there could be a whole new

world waiting to be explored, if we would only venture out

to experience it and wake up our senses.

Always remember to bask under blue skies and sunshine,

Because this adds to our life by recharging and lifting

the spirit.

There is beauty and wisdom in them all and when we learn

to focus on that which is of essence to our life,

we will experience excitement and enrichment

to our soul.

1-00

It is time to take one's power back, when we have been

living within another's mind for far too long.

5-11

One way to deal with most complexities in life, is to step

outside of the event,

and become the silent observer. By doing so we take our

emotions out of the drama

and can clearly focus on a beneficial outcome.

5-11

True joy cannot be bought or it cannot be sold.

It cannot be heard, it cannot be told.

You won't find it elsewhere or outside of yourself.

It's not something you use then set back on the shelf.

We all possess its magic if we look deep within.

It's as easy as staying grounded, in the moment we

are in.

To intensify joy and keep a smile in your heart,

practicing appreciation each day is the best place to

start.

11-10

On our path in life there are many cross roads

to lead us in many directions.

Sometimes we need to veer off the path and head into

unknown territories.

By taking these steps we become trail blazers . . .

and if we walk in peace, love, truth and wisdom the blaze

will keep the path lit so that others may follow.

7-05

Thoughts

Thoughts

CHAPTER TWO

Living

On

Vibrational

Exuberance

Life is a constant growing experience, but when present

circumstances don't permit this, love is also dampened.

Without love, especially for oneself, then joy and

happiness are hard to find.

In some cases, in order to rekindle the love for oneself,

this could require a complete transplant to a new

environment and atmosphere that replenishes the soul.

Enduring some minor pain and setbacks, we can let

our roots take hold in fresh soil, start new growth

and begin to flower anew.

6-98

People who truly know love can speak it,

project it, and act upon it.

Then there are those that just don't get it.

That's so sad for such self-inflicted misery.

9-98

Anyone can be nice . . .

But kindness comes only from a loving heart.

7-11

Take time to,

Treat yourself.

Pamper yourself.

Console yourself.

Comfort yourself.

Healthfully indulge yourself

in all that you love.

By taking the time to love yourself . . .

you won't ever be disappointed.

12-99

When we are with fear, the present moment is lost.

We begin to futurize past experiences; anticipating

something bad to happen. Anxiety, anger, sadness

or even boredom can act as a mask to fear-based emotions.

Where fear resides; love is void. Love becomes

suppressed to seemingly nonexistence. Love can

and will triumph over fear. One only needs to

recapture the sense of spontaneity, the joyful present

quality of innocence and play in any given situation.

This is yet another way to experience love.

5-05

Thoughts of you keep coming into, and

traveling in my mind.

Our moments shared where not long enough,

yet they where divine.

I long for your smile again, to feel your touch

and caring warm embrace.

My soul would soar in ecstasy beyond this

earthly place.

For now I only have thoughts of you for

time and distance keeps us apart.

Although I feel your presence;

you're always in my

heart.

12-05

It is not wise to give our heart to another

person or circumstance, but to only share it.

For only we can keep it replenished with

love.

5-11

Through this love I have learned to be
still and trust divine essence to guide me.
In this love I have learned to honor the
shadow as well as the light, knowing
that each has their place in love's growth.
And when the shadow disappears we
come in contact with soul.
Within this love I have obtained the
knowing of unconditional Love. This is
when one loves so deeply expecting
nothing in return.
Without this love, I would have never
experienced what some think they have
found; what some search a lifetime for
yet never find; what some find and never
let go.

12-03

Love, call it unconditional, call it divine . . .

but in its true sense . . . it goes beyond

family and friends.

It surpasses sexual attraction. It reaches into

the depths of the soul, connecting one to

their higher-self and all else in existence.

In this connection, it is not gender specific

or only towards another human being, but it

encompasses nature with its ever changing

tapestry and ALL the diverse inhabitants

that makes this earth so special.

When one feels this Love it permeates the

whole being giving you a sense of divine

connectedness and a desire to stay with this

vibrational flow of Love.

4-11

Love the highest vibrational force

possible.

Its intensity can literally sweep you

off your feet and take you to places

you can't imagine.

Ahhh . . . the energy of Love.

4-11

Mastering love is when . . .

the

feeling resonates

throughout one's being

by simply thinking of the word . . .

"Love."

5-11

Always

flow

in

the

direction

of

what

you

love.

5-11

CHAPTER THREE

Awareness

Notably

Guiding

Us

In

Spiritual

Hope

Oh, what relentless turmoil of struggle with negative

thoughts that supersedes positive awareness.

The constant expectations of what others feel

we should be or do.

We must learn to stop the merry-go-round process before

we bottom out in the merciless pit of

emotional self-destruction.

Die the death of your old ways, beliefs and conditioning

that no longer suit you. So that you may enjoy the

resurrection of being true to yourself.

1-00

What is this dark lonely place I have stumbled into?

A place where wrestling with fear is a constant struggle

and anxiety lurks in the mist waiting.

At a loss for staying in the moment, while being consumed

with human mortality. Wanting desperately to go back, yet

fully know one can't.

So, I move on trusting in the love of spirit to engulf me and

light my way.

8-04

Sometimes tears are the only release

to suppressed tension, stress, and anxiety.

Let them liberate your body, mind and

spirit.

5-11

Sometimes the mind can't rest it's like a spell I'm under.

Thoughts, feelings and emotions erupt like

bouts of thunder.

The swirling winds what they carry are

exciting and enticing,

spinning me around and round,

trying to change my rigid mind set.

The lightning bolts they flash anxiety and fear.

I want to step outside but only when it's clear.

When did this storm arise has it been brewing for a while?

I long for the sunshine's warm and friendly smile.

4-05

The emptiness and the solitude of the soul

leaves room for new growth but with a price.

When faced with drastic changes, chaos, can

become an all encompassing force.

The heart and mind agrees only to

disagree again and again.

The physical sensation of the fire is no longer felt.

Only the hot ambers under foot remind us to keep moving.

Happiness, sadness, fear, courage, love and hate

all melt together.

One struggles with the restlessness of their being, only to

succumb to what will be.

5-05

Sentences left unfinished . . .

Thoughts left unprocessed . . .

Encouragement no longer there . . .

Questions left unanswered . . .

Genuine caring gone . . .

Unconditional heartfelt love

never to be replaced . . .

This empty feeling, impossible to fill . . .

1-06

In contemplating life, what torment to one's soul;

knowing something more is to be grasped.

Yet, not knowing what or how to make it complete.

In the silence I wait patiently for the answer to be

bestowed upon my soul.

1-00

When disappointments come from the same

situation and person, we are not to internalize it.

Keep your faith.

By realizing that whatever you are being

disappointed about be it opportunity, money, love,

kindness, understanding . . . may not be found there,

remembering that a person who callously disappoints

could have deep seated ego driven disappointments about

themselves.

So take this as a nudge that you will need to

follow your heart's desire elsewhere.

5-11

Dis-ease cannot take root where

love and joy reside.

5-11

CHAPTER FOUR

Special

Earthly

Actions

Sending

Out

New

Sensations

During the winter solstice when everything

is barren, we must remember that nature still

abounds. When we compare this to ourselves,

it's a time for deep inner reflections of our soul,

so we will know what to bring forth to enrich it.

Much like the spring bringing forth new growth.

12-99

On this cold crisp winter day let me bring to mind

all that warms my soul,

all that makes my heart sing with delight,

all that I can add to this web of life so that

peace, love, and harmony can prevail.

2-10

As the old year has passed and the new one begins;

I shall dismiss any thoughts, words, and deeds that

don't project that which is in my best interest.

By letting them fall away they cannot hamper my

progression or another's that I come in contact with

on this earth walk.

I shall enlighten with only positive thoughts, words and

deeds,

not only for myself but for others to benefit from as well.

1-11

On this special spring solstice that entered in

with a 'warm moon,' I will keep in mind all the

new dreams I wish to manifest in my life.

May each and everyone keep in mind their dreams

as if they already own them for then they shall

become your reality.

3-11

Spring a time to make room for new growth not only

in our gardens and homes, but also in our life.

So when cleaning our own personal clutter let us not

forget, our thoughts and emotions.

If it doesn't feel good, release it, so that a new positive

thought or feeling can take its place.

In doing so there will be room to grow.

3-11

OH, the summer solstice . . .

to feel the summer breeze caressing

my face and body.

Gently flowing through my hair like

the finger tips of a close intimate lover.

To be at one with nature and the universe,

the soul becomes intoxicated with the

Blessings and Love of spirit.

Let me savor this time so I may recapture

it at will.

3-00

The fall equinox. What is the revelry with this

time of year?

Is it the crispness of it all, the cool air, and the

fallen leaves?

Or is it the shades of orange, red, and brown grounding us

to Mother Earth.

Let me not explain it, but take pleasure in the

autumn season.

5-11

CHAPTER FIVE

New

Awakings

To

Universal

Radiating

Essences

Try to appreciate all the awesome gifts from God

that have been bestowed upon us.

Like a sunset with warm hues of gold and orange;

A pastel rainbow during a sunny midday rain;

Butterflies flittering; song birds singing their unique

individual song; a moonlit starry night; or any of the

wonders nature provides us with.

When we can acknowledge the beauty and simplicity,

we then will be Blessed with even greater gifts.

6-99

Each day should be like a walk

in a country garden.

You can either hurry through with

your mind preoccupied or you can

casually stroll.

A casual stroll is how it was meant to be enjoyed,

taking in all the colors and fragrances as the

sunlight plays upon them warming the

heart and soul.

Watching the rabbits scurry and play; seeing

the squirrels gather and perform their

acrobatic stunts, hearing the birds sing their

songs of life, and just knowing that everything

is taken care of in its own time.

If we only take the time, every day can be a

Beautiful Day.

7-99

Escape the hustle and the bustle,

replenish your energy by slipping

away with nature, if only for a few

moments. It will rejuvenate your

body, mind and soul.

12-99

NATURE...

The Best Human Energy Resource Available.

Indulge!

12-99

To revel in nature is to be one with God!

1-00

When in doubt shout . . .

I am one with Universe . . .

God will see me through!

1-00

When the clouds are Oh so grey . . .

Let sunshine illuminate from

your heart to brighten up the day.

11-10

How sublime to be brushed by butterfly wings,

tis like a kiss from heaven.

5-06

On this earth walk, let me not miss one God

sent inspiration on my path.

Let me see each morning as a new awakening,

Let me see every tree, flower, stream, animal,

blade of grass, stone and pebble with an awe

for spirit.

Let the warmth of the sun nourish and comfort me.

Let the rain wash away any unwanted thoughts

cleansing my emotions.

Let the cold winter chill stir something new

in my soul.

Let every drifting cloud carry my thoughts and

dreams closer to their destiny.

Let me fulfill the promise for which I am here for.

7-01

A flower blooms in all its Beauty whether

someone is there to appreciate it or not.

5-11

Touch the sky . . .

Feel the earth . . .

Observe and listen to the wonders of nature . . .

Be at one with the universe . . .

Connect to the Magical Essence!

7-11

When one appreciates and loves nature,

a special part of their soul opens.

8-11

Chapter Six

Soul

Permeating

Inspirational

Rays

In

Truth

Fear has no place in our lives,

for when it is present it can

encompass us and cut us off from

truly living. We must be willing to jump

into the abyss and free fall, completely

trusting God and his universal powers

to direct the winds to carry us where we

should be and send us what we need.

6-99

Make each day a Body, Mind, and Spirit day.

Give them all the positive uplifting attention

you can.

1-00

Serenity, Peace, harmony, and Balance

is there for all.

Getting back to nature is one of the easiest

ways to achieve this.

Meditating and freeing one's mind of all

our thoughts, worries and problems is another.

Combining the two is the ultimate healing vibration.

Make time to disconnect and reconnect to

your higher-self.

7-99

When we are overcome by a restless

uneasy feeling that disrupts our life.

This is a sign that our inner being is

dissatisfied.

We must explore what desires have been

dwelling within us our entire life, for the

soul cannot be content till we become our

authentic self.

7-99

When you have that steady gnawing feeling

deep within that there is something you

should be expressing or creating.

It could be the voice of God letting you

know why you are here.

11-99

In every life there are God sent people

who arrive when we are prepared to do

some serious soul work.

They make us realize our soul's potential.

For those that recognize it, they will

understand the Blessing and grasp it,

fearlessly.

So do not let fear hinder your dreams.

11-99

The enchanting moments of life,

sometimes cannot be explained.

Their happening aren't very frequent but,

they move us just the same.

It can happen in a smile, a laugh; or

light conversation.

Like waiting on a breathless morning sunrise

with much anticipation.

The joy a soul does feel from such an

unexpected pleasure, one will notice but never

try to measure.

It happens all again when the mind draws near it.

Maybe this is what happens in the touching of

'Kindred Spirits.'

4-05

Hold on to your Dreams,

they will be yours

when you are ready for them.

12-99

In your most quiet times pay attention to the

messages that are brought to you. This is

God's way of guiding you.

12-99

Dream . . .

Believe it to be true . . .

Enjoy the reward . . .

4-11

Spirituality comes from within.

It is a vibrational force, a way of life

that involves a deep Love and Appreciation

for all God's creations.

5-11

A kindred spirit is always there.

Some how, some way, you know they care.

Their thoughts and actions are from a familiar plane.

They hold a passion for life that is one and the same.

Talking for hours on pleasures and pains.

Breaking down emotional walls helps one feel alive

once again.

When referring to God, they know he is there, cause

the essence of Love penetrates the air.

So how is it kindred? Oh you'll know from the start.

It's the touching of spirit, felt heart to heart.

6-05

The mind is driven by ego but,

the heart is driven by spirit.

5-11

Angels walk amongst us, some say it's

hard to tell.

We need only pay attention and we can feel them

just as well.

They speak to us intuitively when they quickly

come and go.

As we open to their frequency we only then can know.

They guard us and they guide us sometimes through

another human being.

When it comes to higher guidance

remember…

It's all about Believing.

5-11

An angel will always leave you with

a smile in your heart.

5-11

We spend all our life flowing back to the

source.

Only to realize it was meant to be on a river

of love.

5-11

THANKS

I wish to express a heartfelt appreciation to all

those who helped me to make this book possible

and also…

my readers.

Dr. Paula Sekeras N.H.D., Ph.D.

EPILOGUE

By changing the way we think, we change the way we feel.

By changing the way we feel, we change the way we perceive.

By changing the way we perceive, we are able to make better

choices for ourselves and this planet we call home.

14081168R00069

Made in the USA
Lexington, KY
07 March 2012